IT'S GREAT TO BE A FAN IN MINNESOTA

by Matthew McCabe

FOCUS READERS

FOCUS READERS

www.focusreaders.com

Focus Readers is distributed by North Star Editions:
sales@northstareditions.com | 888-417-0195

Produced for Focus Readers by Red Line Editorial.

Photographs ©: Gerry Angus/Icon Sportswire/AP Images, cover (top), 1 (top); Bruce Kluckhohn/AP Images, cover (bottom left), 1 (bottom left); Jim Mone/AP Images, cover (bottom right), 1 (bottom right), 21; photo.ua/Shutterstock Images, 4–5, 7; inese.online/Shutterstock Images, 9; Red Line Editorial, 11, 35; AP Images, 12–13; Gus Ruelas/AP Images, 15; Aaron Lavinsky/Star Tribune/AP Images, 17; Al Messerschmidt/AP Images, 19; Larry Stoddard/AP Images, 23; Ken Wolter/Shutterstock Images, 24–25, 27; Paul Battaglia/AP Images, 28; Ken Felepchuk/Shutterstock Images, 30–31; Josh Holmberg/Icon Sportswire/AP Images, 33; David Berding/Icon Sportswire/AP Images, 37; Dean K./Shutterstock Images, 38–39; Frank Romeo/Shutterstock Images, 43; Mark Herreid/Shutterstock Images, 45

ISBN
978-1-63517-932-3 (hardcover)
978-1-64185-034-6 (paperback)
978-1-64185-236-4 (ebook pdf)
978-1-64185-135-0 (hosted ebook)

Library of Congress Control Number: 2018931999

Printed in the United States of America
Mankato, MN
May, 2018

ABOUT THE AUTHOR

Matthew McCabe has been a freelance writer since 2008. What began as a hobby turned into a career. In addition to writing numerous other titles within series such as Change Makers, he is also a contract marketing and advertising copywriter. He lives in Plymouth, Minnesota, with his wife and two children.

TABLE OF CONTENTS

Minnesota
Welcomes
You

CHAPTER 1

THE LAND OF 10,000 LAKES

Long before Minnesota had a hockey team called the North Stars, the state was known as the "Star of the North." That motto shows the pride Minnesotans take in their state. They feel the same way about the teams that represent it.

Long before Europeans arrived in Minnesota, American Indian tribes called it home. The first tribes settled in what is now Minnesota nearly 9,000 years ago. Europeans arrived in the 1620s.

Minnesota welcomes more than 30 million tourists each year.

Fur was an important resource for both groups. Minnesota's lakes, rivers, and forests were filled with wildlife. French hunters and trappers could sell the fur of certain animals for large amounts of money.

Dakota and Ojibwa tribes lived in the area for generations. French explorers came and went from the region. It was not until 1819 that European-Americans settled in Minnesota permanently. In 1837, the settlers signed a **treaty** with the native tribes. This treaty gave the settlers land to develop. Much of this territory was excellent farmland.

The settlers gained access to land along the Mississippi, St. Croix, and Crow Wing Rivers. American Indians had been farming these areas for centuries. Their primary crops were corn, potatoes, turnips, and pumpkins. In contrast, the

Minnesota's largest city, Minneapolis, is located on the Mississippi River.

white settlers grew mostly potatoes and wheat. They also raised cows to provide milk and fresh meat.

Rivers were hugely important in Minnesota's history. For example, the Mississippi River flows all the way from Lake Itasca in Minnesota to the Gulf of Mexico off the coast of Louisiana. This water highway allowed people in Minnesota to send their products to markets around the world.

Therefore, access to the river played a key role in the **economy**, not just for Minnesota but also for the entire United States.

In the 1800s and early 1900s, the state's economy was dominated by agriculture. Farms produced wheat, potatoes, and other crops. Flour soon became the state's biggest export. In Minneapolis, the West Side Milling District was built in 1858. That was the same year Minnesota became a state.

Flour mills in Minneapolis used water for power. The source of that water was Saint Anthony Falls on the Mississippi River. The flowing water powered the machinery that milled the flour. By the 1890s, Minneapolis had 24 flour mills.

In the mid-1900s, Minnesota's economy began to change. The state still had many farms. But in the cities, companies started to focus

The Minneapolis skyway system keeps people warm even on the coldest winter days.

on manufacturing goods. Today, Minnesota companies produce a variety of computer and electronic products. The state is also one of the top exporters of medical tools.

The city of Minneapolis has changed along with the state's economy. Minneapolis is the largest city in Minnesota. While some mill buildings still exist in Minneapolis, none of them produce flour anymore. Instead, most of the buildings downtown are offices connected by skyways.

The skyway is a system of indoor hallways that allow people to cross streets and move between buildings without going outside.

Although Minneapolis is the state's largest city, it is not the capital. That honor goes to Saint Paul, located just a few miles to the east. Together, Minneapolis and Saint Paul are known as the Twin Cities. As the state's second-largest city, Saint Paul is home to a mixture of large national companies and small Minnesota-based companies. Minnesota's weather, history, and geography impact its sports teams. Taking their

THINK ABOUT IT

Minnesota is known for being cold and snowy, with approximately 70 inches (178 cm) of snow annually. How do you think Minnesota's earliest inhabitants survived the harsh cold?

name from the Twin Cities, the Twins enjoy warm summers playing baseball outdoors. In contrast, the Vikings play football indoors to avoid the freezing winter temperatures.

MAP OF PRO STADIUMS IN MINNEAPOLIS–SAINT PAUL

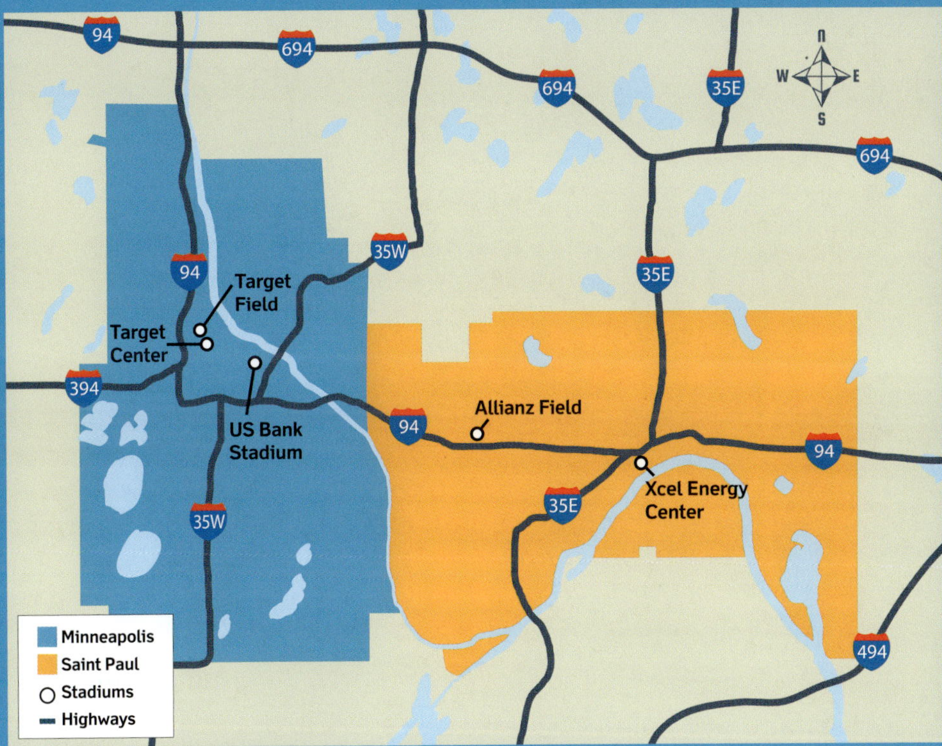

LAKERS
99

CHAPTER 2

SMALL MARKET, MAJOR ACCOMPLISHMENTS

Compared to other areas in the United States, Minneapolis–Saint Paul is a relatively small market. In professional sports, *small market* refers to regions that have a smaller population, meaning there is a smaller number of fans who watch and attend games. Despite being a small market, Minnesota has six professional sports teams. The state has one team in each of North America's four major sports leagues.

The Twin Cities now enjoy teams in all professional sports, but basketball was first.

The Twin Cities are one of only 12 American markets with that status.

Hockey may be Minnesota's most popular sport, but basketball is what turned Minnesota into a major-league state. Minnesota's first professional sports team was the Minneapolis Lakers. The team entered the National Basketball Association (NBA) in 1948. The team was named the Lakers because of the state's nickname. Minnesota is known as the Land of 10,000 Lakes. The Minneapolis Lakers were the first **dynasty** in NBA history. Between 1949 and 1954, the team won five titles in six seasons.

The Lakers moved to Los Angeles, California, in 1960. But since then, Minnesota has gotten two new basketball teams. The Minnesota Timberwolves entered the NBA as a new franchise in 1989.

Kevin Garnett led the Timberwolves on their playoff run in 2003–04.

The best season in Timberwolves history came in 2003–04. The team won its first playoff series in eight tries. The Timberwolves made it all the way to the Western Conference Finals but lost in six games.

The new basketball dynasty in Minnesota is the Lynx. The Lynx play in the Women's National Basketball Association (WNBA). Founded in 1999, the Lynx won just a single playoff game in their first decade of existence. But starting in 2011, they won four of the next seven WNBA titles.

Minnesota's oldest and most popular teams both began play in 1961. The Minnesota Vikings entered the National Football League (NFL) that season. They struggled through some early losing seasons, but by the late 1960s they had developed a legendary defense. The Vikings defense, known as the Purple People Eaters, led the team to the 1969 NFL Championship.

The Vikings then played in their first Super Bowl, where they were heavy favorites. However, the underdog Kansas City Chiefs won the game. The Vikings appeared in three more Super Bowls

Led by league Most Valuable Player Sylvia Fowles, the Lynx won their fourth WNBA title in 2017.

in the 1970s. Despite a strong defense and Hall of Fame quarterback Fran Tarkenton, the Vikings lost all of the Super Bowls they appeared in.

One of the greatest Vikings teams of all time didn't even make it to the Super Bowl. The 1998 team had a historically great offense, led by Hall of Fame wide receiver Randy Moss.

The 1998 Vikings lost just a single game in the regular season and made it to the conference championship game. But they lost in overtime to the Atlanta Falcons in another upset.

Baseball is also popular in Minnesota. The Twins are the state's Major League Baseball (MLB) team. The franchise began as the Washington Senators in 1901. When the team moved to Minnesota in 1961, the roster was filled with young talent. These players helped the Twins reach the World Series by 1965, but they fell to the Los Angeles Dodgers in seven games.

A new generation of players redeemed the team by winning two thrilling World Series in 1987 and 1991. Hall of Fame outfielder Kirby Puckett was a favorite of Twins fans. His game-winning home run in Game 6 of the 1991 series was one of the greatest moments in team

Vikings wide receiver Randy Moss set an NFL rookie record with 17 touchdowns in 1998.

history. The Twins then won the next night in Game 7 to win their second title in four seasons.

Hockey is perhaps the sport that Minnesotans love most. Pro hockey first came to Minnesota in 1967. That year, the Minnesota North Stars entered the National Hockey League (NHL).

The team was named after the state motto, L'Etoile du Nord, which is French for "Star of the North." The North Stars played in Minnesota for 26 seasons. In that time, they reached two Stanley Cup Finals, losing both. In 1993, the team moved to Dallas, Texas, and became known as the Dallas Stars.

Today, the Minnesota Wild are the state's NHL team. The Wild play their home games in Saint Paul. The team joined the NHL as an expansion team in 2000. After just three seasons, the Wild reached the Western Conference Finals. This memorable run ended in a loss to the Anaheim Ducks.

The newest pro team in Minnesota plays soccer. Minnesota United joined Major League Soccer (MLS) in 2017. The team is unofficially known as the Loons. The loon is the state bird of Minnesota,

Minnesotans love their hockey. The Wild sold out the first 409 home games in team history.

and the team uses a loon in its logo. The use of the loon is just one example of how Minnesota's sports teams represent their state with pride.

DAVE WINFIELD

Dave Winfield was born in Saint Paul in 1951. He is one of Minnesota's greatest hometown athletes. He grew up playing several different sports, but baseball and basketball were his best. As a young athlete, Winfield went to the University of Minnesota. He earned a **scholarship** there for his athletic skills. He played both baseball and basketball at the U of M. He was an outfielder and pitcher for the Gophers in 1973 when the team reached the College World Series. When he finished college, Winfield became the first and only athlete **drafted** by four teams.

The Minnesota Vikings drafted Winfield for football. The San Diego Padres drafted him for baseball. Two basketball teams drafted him in the American Basketball Association (ABA). One was the Atlanta Hawks, and the other the Utah Stars.

Dave Winfield was a standout pitcher and outfielder for the University of Minnesota.

Winfield spent his pro career in baseball. He never played in the minors, going right to the Padres' major league roster. He played in the majors for 23 seasons. He played more than 1,100 games with both San Diego and the New York Yankees. In 1993, Winfield came back home and played for the Minnesota Twins, where he collected his 3,000th career hit. He was inducted into the National Baseball Hall of Fame in 2001.

CHAPTER 3

THE GOPHER STATE

Minnesota is known as the Gopher State. The name comes from an 1857 **political cartoon** about railroad construction. In the cartoon, several gophers are pulling a train along the tracks. The gopher nickname stuck, and before long it was being used by the largest university in the state. The University of Minnesota's main campus has more than 50,000 students. Its sports teams are known as the Golden Gophers.

The University of Minnesota is spread across two campuses in Minneapolis and Saint Paul.

The university's most popular spectator sports include football, basketball, and hockey.

The Gophers football team played its first game in 1882. In its long history, the team has won seven national championships. The first title came in 1904. The Gophers won three titles in a row from 1934 to 1936, which hasn't been done in **Division I** since. They added two more in 1940 and 1941. The last national title came in 1960. Bernie Bierman was the head coach for five of the Gophers' national titles. He led the team for 16 years and has the second-most wins in school history with 93.

Gophers men's and women's basketball have both had periods of success. The men's team made back-to-back Sweet Sixteen appearances in 1989 and 1990. And Hall of Famer Kevin McHale played for the Gophers from 1976 to 1980.

The Golden Gophers football team opened TCF Bank Stadium in 2009 with a win over Air Force.

But the Gopher women have had much more recent success. Led by future Lynx star Lindsay Whalen, the Gophers went to the Final Four in 2004. Whalen's jersey No. 13 was retired by the Gophers the next year.

Minnesota men's hockey has produced numerous NHL players, such as Blake Wheeler.

But there is no sport the Gophers have had more success in than hockey. The University of Minnesota has two elite hockey programs. The men's team dates back to the 1921–22 season and has won five national championships.

The Gophers won three of their championships in the 1970s under the leadership of head coach

Herb Brooks. The team's all-time winningest head coach is Don Lucia. He led the team to national titles in 2002 and 2003. And as of 2018, the Gophers have won the most games in the history of men's college hockey.

Gopher women's hockey is also a source of school and state pride. The women's team started in 1997. Since then, they have won more than 600 games. The team won nine conference titles and seven national titles in its first 20 years. Both the men's and women's teams have their own arenas on campus and draw large numbers of hockey fans.

THINK ABOUT IT

The University of Minnesota is one of just 34 Division I schools to have both men's and women's hockey. Why do you think every school does not have both?

CHAPTER 4

THE STATE OF HOCKEY

Minnesota has many nicknames, but perhaps none holds more pride than the State of Hockey. The weather in Minnesota is cold in winter, so playing games on icy ponds is a natural fit. According to USA Hockey, no state has more hockey players than Minnesota. In 2014, approximately 54,000 Minnesota kids were signed up to play. Next was Michigan with 50,000. And Michigan has twice the population of Minnesota.

Outdoor hockey is a popular winter activity in Minnesota.

At all levels, Minnesota kids love hockey. The state high school hockey tournament is extremely popular. Students, parents, and regular hockey fans attend the Minnesota State High School League tournament each March. The tournament is held in Saint Paul at the home of the Wild. Schools are split into two classes (A and AA) by **enrollment**. Tickets, especially for the AA tournament, can be hard to come by.

In 2017, more than 100,000 people attended the games. Even more impressive was the TV audience. Viewers watched the Minnesota high school hockey tournament from all over, including all 50 states and 37 different countries.

College hockey is also very popular in Minnesota. The state has five teams that play Division I college hockey. The Golden Gophers have been around the longest.

Edina is the most successful high school hockey program in Minnesota, with 12 state championships as of 2018.

As one of college hockey's greatest programs, the Gophers could recruit players from almost anywhere. But the Gophers have an unofficial tradition of preferring Minnesota players to fill their roster. And there is enough talent in the state to do so.

In fact, the state has enough talent to sustain four other Division I programs: St. Cloud State University; Minnesota State University, Mankato; the University of Minnesota Duluth; and Bemidji State University. Minnesota produces the most NHL players of any state. By 2018, more than 250 Minnesotans had played in the NHL.

Minnesota hockey has even had international success. The 1980 men's Olympic team won a game that came to be known as the Miracle on Ice and went on to win the gold medal. Of the team's 20 players, 13 were born in Minnesota.

The tiny northern town of Eveleth is home to the United States Hockey Hall of Fame. Even though Eveleth has fewer than 4,000 residents, nine NHL players were born there. The State of Hockey is more than just a name. Hockey is a major part of Minnesota culture.

MAP OF NCAA DIVISION I HOCKEY PROGRAMS IN MINNESOTA

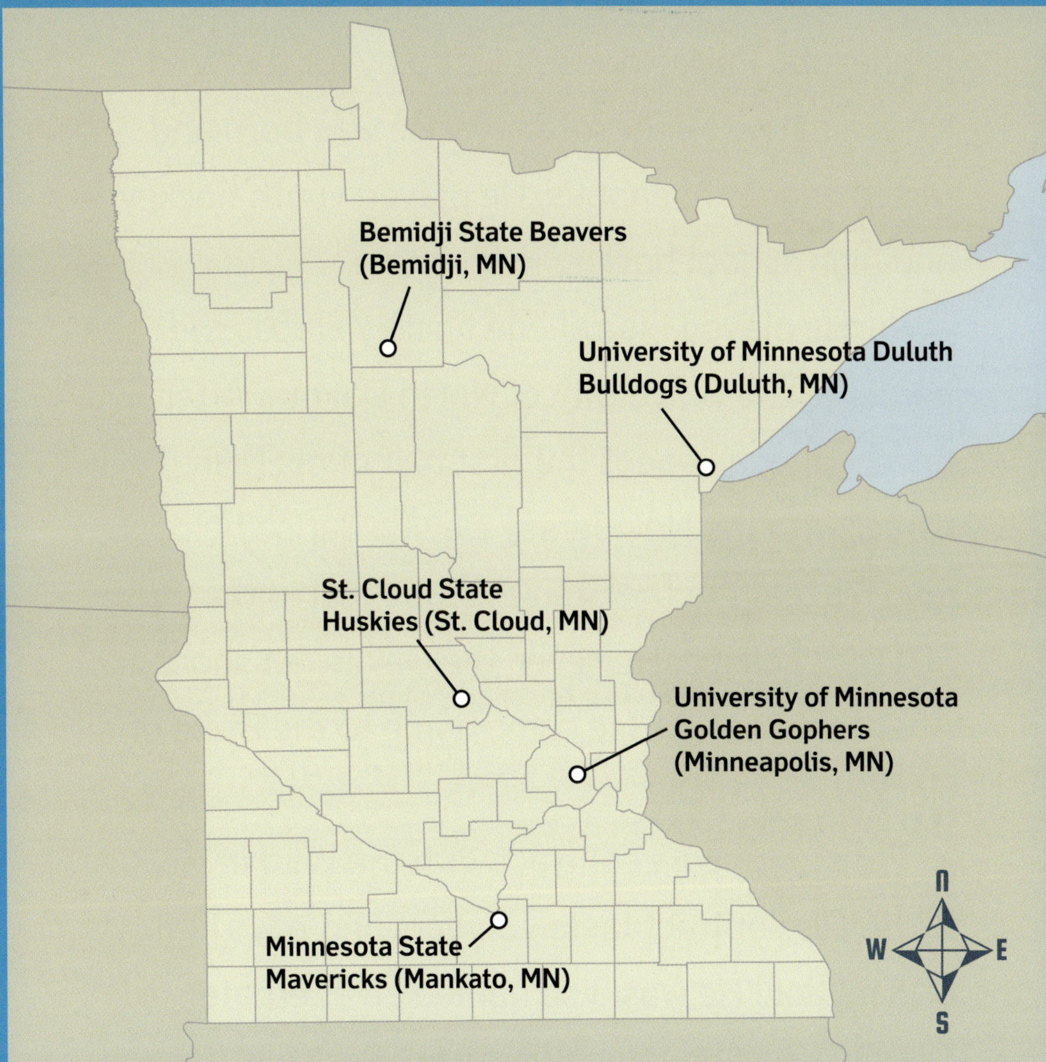

ZACH PARISE

Zach Parise could be called hockey royalty in Minnesota. Parise doesn't just play for the Wild. He is a native Minnesotan. Parise was born and raised near Minneapolis. He played youth hockey and high school hockey in the state.

Parise played his college hockey across the border at the University of North Dakota. After turning pro, he spent the first half of his NHL career with the New Jersey Devils. Parise helped lead his team to the Stanley Cup Final in the 2011–12 season. However, the Devils fell short. After that loss, Parise came home to the State of Hockey.

Parise signed a contract with the Wild in 2012. His contract lasts 13 years and pays him $98 million. He was also named an alternate captain when he joined the team. Parise is a tough

Zach Parise is an alternate captain with his hometown Minnesota Wild.

player known for his nonstop work ethic on the ice. He plays hard and is always around the net.

Parise's father, J. P., spent time in the NHL as well. He played for the Minnesota North Stars in the 1960s and 1970s and later was an assistant coach. Prior to his death in 2015, J. P. regularly attended Wild home games to cheer for his son.

CHAPTER 5

MINNESOTA NICE OR MINNESOTA ICE?

People who visit Minnesota often describe the locals as polite and friendly. This characteristic, which is often referred to as Minnesota Nice, can be traced back to the **heritage** of the state's residents. Minnesota is known as the Norwegian capital of the United States. In fact, more than 800,000 Minnesotans have Norwegian ancestors. There are also 500,000 people with Swedish ancestors.

A statue of Norwegian explorer Leif Erikson in Duluth honors Minnesota's Scandinavian roots.

The cultures of these countries came to Minnesota along with immigrants. Minnesota Nice points to the kind behavior of Minnesotans. Most make friends relatively slowly, but they tend to keep those friends for life.

Minnesota gained more than culture from Norway and Sweden. One of the state's most prominent teams is the Minnesota Vikings, which takes its name from Scandinavian history. Vikings were fierce warriors who took on any enemy. Therefore, it made sense to give the NFL team that name, as it reflects the state's culture and geography.

The state of Minnesota is one of the coldest in the country. In fact, the city of International Falls is sometimes called the Icebox of the Nation. The city regularly sets records for cold weather. In fact, it has been ranked as one of the five coldest places on Earth. International Falls is located in northern Minnesota, just across the Rainy River from Ontario, Canada. The winter of 2013–2014 set new records for the city of International Falls.

COLDEST CITIES IN THE NATION

4 Minnesota cities in top 15 (min. population 10,000)

Duluth, Minnesota (5)	St. Cloud, Minnesota (7)
Average monthly minimum temperature: 1.5 degrees Fahrenheit (–16.9°C) Average monthly maximum temperature: 55.4 degrees Fahrenheit (13.0°C) Average annual snowfall: 81.5 inches (207.0 cm)	Average monthly minimum temperature: 1.8 degrees Fahrenheit (–16.8°C) Average monthly maximum temperature: 58.4 degrees Fahrenheit (14.7°C) Average annual snowfall: 44.9 inches (114.0 cm)
Minneapolis–Saint Paul, Minnesota (12)	**Rochester, Minnesota (14)**
Average monthly minimum temperature: 7.5 degrees Fahrenheit (–13.6°C) Average monthly maximum temperature: 64.1 degrees Fahrenheit (17.8°C) Average annual snowfall: 50.4 inches (128.0 cm)	Average monthly minimum temperature: 7.7 degrees Fahrenheit (–13.5°C) Average monthly maximum temperature: 61.3 degrees Fahrenheit (16.3°C) Average annual snowfall: 49.6 inches (126.0 cm)

The coldest temperature recorded that winter was –42 degrees Fahrenheit (–41°C). And in December, the city spent eight days below –30 degrees Fahrenheit (–34°C). All that cold makes Minnesota a great place for hockey. The state's 10,000 lakes are frozen for much of the winter.

Minnesota's sports facilities have had a big impact on the state. The Twin Cities are home to several stadiums and arenas built since 2000. The Xcel Energy Center, which opened in 2000, holds more than 18,000 people. In addition to being the home of the Wild, the arena also hosts high school and college tournaments, plus many concerts. The Lynx even used it as a temporary home in 2017 when they won the WNBA title.

TCF Bank Stadium in Minneapolis is the home of Gopher football. Opened in 2009, it seats approximately 50,000. Minnesota United FC also

Target Field, home of the Minnesota Twins, offers a spectacular view of downtown Minneapolis.

played its first two seasons there while its own stadium, Allianz Field in Saint Paul, was being built. TCF Bank Stadium also hosts many outdoor concerts in the spring and summer months. Similar to football games, these concerts have a significant effect on the local economy.

The Minnesota Twins play outdoors at Target Field. Built specifically for baseball, the park opened in 2010 and seats approximately 40,000.

The Twins play 81 home games there each season. Target Field also hosted the 2014 MLB All-Star Game.

US Bank Stadium, which opened in 2016, is home to the Minnesota Vikings. The stadium is the largest in the state. It seats approximately 66,000 people and cost more than $1.1 billion to build. In addition to hosting the 2018 Super Bowl, it was chosen to host the 2019 NCAA Final Four.

These new venues are part of the reason the Twin Cities have been chosen to host so many high-profile events. The area's public transportation network is another reason. All of the stadiums are linked by **light rail** trains. These trains run on tracks set on or near city streets, connecting neighborhoods across Minneapolis and Saint Paul. The longest line is the Green Line. It has stops at Target Field, Target Center, US

US Bank Stadium replaced the Metrodome as the home of the Minnesota Vikings.

Bank Stadium, TCF Bank Stadium, Allianz Field, and Xcel Energy Center. That means visitors can easily get to sporting events on trains. This cuts down on the number of cars on the streets and helps people reach their destination more quickly.

Minnesotans are loyal to one another and to their sports teams. No matter the season, no matter the weather, they'll be out there enjoying all the state has to offer.

FOCUS ON
MINNESOTA

Write your answers on a separate piece of paper.

1. Write a sentence that explains the main ideas of Chapter 5.

2. Do you think Minnesota's climate has influenced the state's success in sports? Why or why not?

3. How many NBA titles did the Minneapolis Lakers win?

- **A.** one
- **B.** three
- **C.** five

4. Why did the Senators change their name after moving to Minnesota?

- **A.** The name made sense in Washington, DC, but it had no connection to Minnesota.
- **B.** People in Washington, DC, voted to make the team change its name.
- **C.** The state of Minnesota did not have any senators at the time.

Answer key on page 48.

GLOSSARY

Division I
The top level of college sports in the United States.

drafted
Chosen by a team when entering a sports league.

dynasty
A team that has a long run of winning championships.

economy
A system of goods, services, money, and jobs.

enrollment
The number of people signed up for something, typically at a school or college.

heritage
Something possessed as a result of one's natural situation or birth.

light rail
A train transportation system for passengers throughout a city.

political cartoon
A simple drawing that comments on a political issue in a funny way.

scholarship
Money given to a student to pay for educational expenses.

treaty
An official agreement between groups.

TO LEARN MORE

BOOKS

Brill, Marlene Targ, and Elizabeth Kaplan. *Minnesota: The Land of 10,000 Lakes*. New York: Cavendish Square, 2014.

Reed, Taylor. *Minnesota Wild*. New York: AV2 by Weigl, 2015.

Whiting, Jim. *Minnesota Timberwolves*. Mankato, MN: Creative Education, Creative Paperbacks, 2018.

NOTE TO EDUCATORS

Visit **www.focusreaders.com** to find lesson plans, activities, links, and other resources related to this title.

INDEX

Answer Key: 1. Answers will vary; **2.** Answers will vary; **3.** C; **4.** A